ISBN: 1492912891
ISBN-13: 978-1492912897

The Leadership Principles of The Republican Party

Ben F. Lynn

DEDICATION

To those who have a political sense of duty, who place themselves in the public eye as servants to the people who will at some point poke fun at their service in the spirit of entertainment and profit.

-Ben Frank Lynn

CONTENTS

ACKNOWLEDGMENTS

Inspired by those who enjoy the American Rights to Freedom of Speech. This book is only made possible by the right to artistic freedom of expression. We thank those who have made it possible to maintain those rights and the protections they grant every American, Especially those with a sense of humor and an understanding of free enterprise and economic stimulation.

YOU WILL NOTE THAT THIS BOOK IS
FULL OF BLANK LINES.

_____

_____

IF YOU DON'T FIND THE HUMOR IN IT,
PLEASE ACCEPT THE LEADERSHIP
CHALLENGE BY FILLING IN THE
BLANK SPACE WITH YOUR OWN
LEADERSHIP PRINCIPLES OR YOUR
PERCIEVED PRINCIPLES OF THE PARTY
OF YOUR CHOOSING.

ONCE YOU HAVE FILLED IT IN, YOU
CAN RE GIFT IT, OR ENTER IT INTO OUR
CONTEST TO HAVE YOUR LEADERSHIP
THOUGHTS PUBLISHED BY DEBONAIRE
PUBLISHING.

WWW.10MILLIONLEADERS.COM FOR
CONTEST DETAILS

ABOUT THE AUTHOR

Ben F. Lynn or commonly known as Ben Frank Lynn is a sharp ol' character with a tongue in cheek view of the world. The constant entrepreneur Ben Is always looking to make a few hundred dollar bills so he can help stimulate the economy by spending them on random stuff, including food, travel and fun. Ben likes to give money to organizations that help people however he does not support brainwashing or manipulation of the system or people.

Mr. Lynn would like to see world peace and all of the people living in hope and prosperity.